New Yacht
The legal aspects

Edmund Whelan
Barrister
and
Mandy Peters
F.Inst.L.Ex

Published by
The Royal Yachting Association
RYA House Ensign Way Hamble
Southampton SO31 4YA

Tel: 0845 345 0400
Fax: 0845 345 0329
Email: info@rya.org.uk
Web: www.rya.org.uk

British Cataloguing in Publication Date:
A Catalogue record of this book is available from the British Library.
ISBN:
Photographic credits: Phil Pickin/Photo-grafix.co.uk,Boat-Pics

© 2004

All rights reserved. No part of this publication may be transmitted,
stored in a retrieval system, or transmitted, in any form or by any means,
electronic, mechanical, photocopying, recording or otherwise, without the
prior permission of the publisher

Note: While all reasonable care has been taken in the preparation of this
book, the publisher takes no responsibility for the use of the methods or
products or contracts described in the book.

CONTENTS

		Page
INTRODUCTION		
1	BASIC LEGAL PRINCIPLES	2
2	STATUTORY PROTECTION FOR YACHT BUYERS	3
3	BUYING A PRODUCTION YACHT	6
4	BUYING THROUGH AN AGENT OR A LEASING SCHEME	11
5	CONSTRUCTION OF A NEW YACHT TO ORDER	13
6	BUYING FOR OVERSEAS DELIVERY	17
7	RECREATIONAL CRAFT DIRECTIVE	19
8	INSURANCE	21
9	REGISTRATION	25
10	OBTAINING A MOORING	30

Appendixes

1	Points to check before signing contract	31
2	BMF/RYA boat building contract	33
3	Draft letter of indemnity from builder on agency purchase	49
4	2004 European Community VAT rates	50

BASIC LEGAL PRINCIPLES

British law says clearly that a yacht owned by a British citizen is a British ship, even if it is not registered. A ship takes the nationality of its owner, and legally speaking a ship is defined as *every description of vessel used in navigation.* So whether you have a small dinghy or an ocean going liner, it can be a British ship.

A large ship is subject to complex legal requirements, but a dinghy to virtually none, except when used on inland waterways in which case a licence must be obtained from the appropriate authority. Yachts can generally be owned and used in UK waters without any special formalities, although you may choose to register your yacht.

The Maritime and Coastguard Agency regards as a private pleasure yacht any pleasure craft used solely for the private purposes of the owner. Yachts used for charter or sailing schools are however subject to a number of construction and equipment rules.

If you are thinking of buying a new or second-hand craft for sailing school or charter use, you would be well advised to consult the RYA or the Yacht Charter Association for specific advice in good time before a purchase agreement is made. The Maritime and Coastguard Agency has strict rules for all yachts intended for commercial use.

Also, if proposing to buy a new craft for use on inland waters, particularly those under the control of the British Waterways Board, the Environment Agency, or the Broads Authority, you should ensure that it will be built and equipped to Boat Safety Scheme standards. If a second hand craft is being purchased, you should ensure that it has a valid certificate of compliance from the appropriate navigation authority.

STATUTORY PROTECTION FOR YACHT BUYERS

Although the investment in a new yacht may be as much as, or more than, a large house, the legal formalities required can be as simple as buying a bicycle. In the case of a new unregistered yacht no special form of contract is required and in contrast to the transfer of land the legal profession does not publish any form of standard contract for sale.

A yacht, of whatever value, is a chattel within the meaning of the Sale of Goods Act 1979 as amended by The Sale and Supply of Goods Act 1994, and a private purchaser will have all the protection afforded to private consumers by that Act. The most important sections from the yacht buyer's point of view are as follows:-

Section 12

Imposes an implied condition in every contract that the seller has a right to sell the goods. If he is not the lawful owner, or a third party has an interest in the goods, (e.g. a marine mortgage) the Act will protect the buyer whether or not the seller knew of his defective title, and the buyer will be entitled to recover his purchase price and damages from the seller (if he can be traced).

Section 13

Imposes an implied condition that, where goods are sold by description, any inaccuracy amounting to a *material misdescription* will give the right to repudiate the contract or to claim damages. This section would be relevant to the purchaser of a vessel where for example the agreed specification was changed without notice. Even if the seller is willing and able to carry out work to rectify the complaint, the consumer is still entitled to repudiate the agreement (unless the complaint is of a minimal or trivial nature).

Section 14

Repeats the old common law rule of Caveat Emptor (let the buyer beware) subject to provisions that goods sold in the course of a trade or business must be of satisfactory quality and fit for the purpose for which they are required. In effect satisfactory quality means being as fit *for the purpose... for which goods of that kind are commonly bought as it is reasonable to expect having regard to any description applied to them, the price (if relevant) and all the other relevant circumstances.* The seller is not held to guarantee that the goods are absolutely suitable, but even a minor defect making the goods unfit will give the buyer the chance to reject the goods so long as he does so in good time. For example the main inland navigation authorities have stringent construction and equipment standards under the Boat Safety Scheme. If, to the knowledge of the seller, the boat is being bought with those standards in mind and it fails to pass the scrutiny of the authority's inspector, the buyer is entitled to repudiate the contract unless the defect is really trivial. Alternatively the buyer may either claim damages or accept an offer by the seller to remedy the defect.

In dealing with cases under the Sale of Goods Act there are two important principles to remember. First, do not delay in pursuing your rights; if you do not act immediately on discovering a defect the court may decide that you have accepted the fault, or you may be judged to have had enough use to prejudice your rights to full redress. Second, always pursue your complaint against the seller, not against the builder, supplier, sailmaker, engine manufacturer, sparmaker etc. (unless they happen to be the same person). Do not be put off by the seller referring you back to the manufacturer of a piece of machinery or equipment; the seller is the only one under a direct obligation under the Sale of Goods Act to put matters right.

You need only be concerned with additional guarantees provided by component makers if the seller of the goods himself is unable to satisfy his contractual obligations.

This does not mean of course that the seller may not arrange for the repair to be carried out by the person best qualified to do so particularly in the case of specialised equipment.

Misrepresentation Act 1967

This Act provides that any misrepresentation about the standard, quality or specification of goods, whether made innocently, negligently or fraudulently, may entitle the buyer either to rescind the contract or to claim damages according to whether the misrepresentation was made innocently, negligently or fraudulently.

A seller must therefore be careful not to make unsustainable specific claims about a yacht's performance, whether as to engine performance, fuel consumption, sailing ability etc. Even with new yachts there is great scope for misunderstandings between salesman and customer, and the buyer is always in a strong position if misleading statements have been made either in writing (e.g. brochures, websites, etc) or verbally in front of witnesses.

BUYING A PRODUCTION YACHT

When buying a series produced yacht the contract may be either direct with the builder or through an agent.

In an ideal world of unbroken promises, solvent builders and prompt deliveries there would be no need for a written contract to define the rights and liabilities of the parties. There is however so much scope for disagreement, misunderstanding and flawed recollection of what was agreed between parties that a written contract is generally regarded as essential.

The terms of the contract offered to potential buyers vary enormously from one builder to another. Every agreement involves a degree of compromise, and it is essential to take a close look at the proposed terms before any commitment is made.

So far as the buyer is concerned, the ideal contract would provide a fixed date for delivery with no stage payments being required, property (i.e. legal ownership) in the yacht passing immediately upon the order being placed, and a full season's sea trials and testing before the final installment is paid.

An ideal contract from the seller's point of view would provide for immediate payment of the full price, no fixed date for delivery, property in the yacht being retained until delivery, and no need for acceptance trials or testing.

In practice neither approach could be regarded as realistic but it is worth detailing some of the more important provisions that should be incorporated in every contract.

Restriction of contract

Some standard form contracts will provide words to the effect that: *No other agreement, representation, promise, undertaking or understanding of any kind unless expressly confirmed in writing by the company shall add to, vary or waive any of these terms or conditions.* Normally this would not be objectionable because it does not invalidate your statutory rights. But this sort of clause should be deleted if a purchase is being made on the strength of promises by a salesman (e.g. about the yacht's performance). A purchaser would be wise to insist on any such promises (e.g. this yacht will achieve x knots at y gph in flat water, or x knots to windward in y knots of true wind in flat water, or compliance with a river authority's or a foreign country's technical requirements) being put in writing together with a statement to the following effect:

> It is expressly agreed that these additional conditions represent a further agreement as required under Clause ... of our Standard terms and conditions and where inconsistent shall prevail notwithstanding those terms and conditions.

Payment and passing of property

In recent years several well-known companies in the yachting industry have gone into receivership, often with considerable debts, some resulting in customers losing large amounts of money with no legal remedy. Where a boatyard with a number of part built yachts on the site calls in a receiver, his first action in assessing the value of the stock and work in progress of the company will be to examine the contracts and decide where ownership of the yachts in question lies. The British Marine Federation standard form agreement provides as follows:

The boat and/or all materials and equipment purchased or appropriated from time to time by the Builders specifically for its construction (whether in their premises, upon the water or elsewhere) shall become the property of the Purchaser upon the payment of the first Stage Payment, or if later, upon the date of the said purchase or appropriation. The Builders shall, however, have a lien on the boat and any materials and equipment for or appropriated to the construction for the recovery of all sums due (whether invoiced or not) under the terms of this Agreement or any variation or modification hereof. Any materials or equipment rejected by the Purchaser shall forthwith revest in the Builders.

In the event of liquidation or receivership therefore, the purchaser of a part-built boat is to some extent protected against the possibility of the part built yacht going into the receiver's general compensation fund. An additional precaution (required by paragraph 11.2 of the agreement) is for the builder to agree to mark all bought-in machinery and equipment with the name of the relevant yacht to enable easy identification in the case of a liquidation.

Of course if a deposit has only just been paid, and no work has yet started on the yacht, the deposit will be lost, so it is essential to pay by way of deposit no more than the buyer could

reasonably afford to loose (typically deposits or first stage payments should be no more than 5% - 10%). Some contracts (or special Boat Show deals) ask for up to 100% before you obtain title; in those situations you could lose the lot.

In contrast to the BMF standard form agreement, some boat builders propose in their contracts that: *Until the company has received full payment for the craft the property in the craft shall remain vested in the company;* or words to that effect. Where the purchase price is divided into a small (say 5%) initial payment and one single final payment of the balance on delivery, this is perhaps not objectionable. Where a larger payment is required, typically one third of the total price, the purchaser is then at considerable risk until the boat is completed and the final installment paid. Where a would-be purchaser is confronted with such a contract he should insist either on the substitution of the BMF wording referred to above or the provision by the builder of a banker's guarantee. This should provide that, in the event of the builder having a receiver or manager appointed, or a petition or resolution to wind up the company, or performing any act of bankruptcy or proposing an arrangement with his creditors, the full amount of all money paid under the contract should immediately be refunded to the purchaser.

If the builder is unwilling to discuss either of these options then the purchaser will have to decide for himself whether to take the very real risk of putting down a deposit and part payment without any protection. If the builder agrees to amend the passing of property clause, he must also undertake to inform his insurance underwriters of the purchaser's interest, otherwise his builder's risks policy may be invalidated, and the buyer should ask for confirmation from the insurers that this has been done.

Building risks insurance

From the moment the property in the yacht passes to you, so will the risk. Thus insurance of some form is required. Normally this will be offered as part of the builder's overall yard insurance, but you may wish to make your own alternative arrangements or at least check with the builders that their insurance cover is adequate.

Damages for late delivery

Paragraph 6 of the contract does not impose any financial burden on the builder if he allows the delivery date to slip. Even though Schedule 3 of the contract provides a firm delivery date and place, this again imposes no financial pressure on the builder, and some buyers may wish to exert additional leverage by inserting an extra paragraph as 6.4 to the following effect:

> *If, due to the builder's failure without reasonable cause to proceed with reasonable dispatch, the craft is not completed by the date agreed .... the builders shall pay the purchaser £.... in respect of each week or part of a week until the craft is completed as agreed damages for loss of use of the craft.*

The figure to be inserted is for agreement between the parties. In many cases the builder may refuse to consent to this; as an alternative it may be possible to agree that the clause should only start to operate after a fixed number of weeks beyond the delivery date. The final form of agreement will depend on how important the delivery date is to the buyer, and how confident the builder is that he can comply with that date. In any event, the builder may well wish to increase the price to allow for the potential risk to him of agreeing this clause.

Arbitration clause

The BMF standard form agreement provides that:

> *If during the construction of the boat any dispute arises either as to an adjustment of the Contract Price pursuant to Clause 3.3 or as to when a Stage Payment is due and payable or as to the operation or duration of a delaying event or whether for the purposes of the policy of insurance the boat has suffered substantial damage then, and without prejudice to the Parties' rights to litigate such dispute, it may be referred to a single surveyor who shall be independent of the Builders and the Purchaser and whose identity and terms of reference shall be agreed by the Parties or, in default of agreement, by the President for the time being of the Yacht Designers and Surveyors Association. The surveyor so appointed shall act as an expert and not as an arbitrator and his written decision shall be final and binding upon the Parties and his fees and expenses shall be borne equally by the Parties.*

Since litigation, even at County Court level, can be a relatively costly process the inclusion of an arbitration clause can be of great importance providing the purchaser with a quick, inexpensive and simple means of resolving certain categories of dispute with the builder.

Acceptance trial

Although an acceptance trial is normally provided for a one-off rather than a series-produced yacht, nonetheless unless the builder actually produces all its yachts off a production line to an identical specification, it makes sense to retain part of the purchase price (typically 5% or 10%) until after the buyer has had a reasonable opportunity to test the yacht in suitable conditions (i.e. not a flat calm), to give the engine, gearbox and drive shaft a good run, to ensure the rig and sail handling systems work in practice, and to test all optional extra equipment by itself and while other equipment is in use (e.g. beware the effect on your GPS of an unshielded microwave oven or a high powered battery charging circuit.).

The standard BMF agreement provides for the purchaser to be given at least 14 days notice of the readiness of the craft for an acceptance trial on a stated date with the proviso (paragraph 5.5) that if the purchaser or his agent fails to appear for the trial then the trial will be deemed to have taken place and to have been satisfactory.

The fact that an acceptance trial is satisfactory and that defects on the craft do not come to light until later does not mean that the purchaser has no remedy. As we have seen, he has a number of statutory rights which cannot be affected by any provisions to the contrary in the contract.

BUYING THROUGH AN AGENT OR A LEASING SCHEME

Although many yacht builders deal direct with their customers, the situation often arises where prospective purchasers, especially those living at a great distance from the builder, will be told after initial inquiry to conduct negotiations and all further business through a local agent. This is increasingly the practice adopted when purchasing yachts from other EU member states.

On the face of it, this seems a perfectly sensible arrangement; the agent knows the local conditions and, furthermore, is able to sort out problems without delay. The purchaser will also be reassured that he is dealing with a locally known personality rather than a distant sales manager.

However, a number of incidents have highlighted a potential danger in purchasing a new yacht through an agent. In one case the yacht concerned was found to have a defective resin mix over part of the hull and in another case a fault in the hull/keel joint. When the owners sought the assistance of the agents from whom they had bought the yacht they found they had gone into liquidation. In one case the owner then asked the builder concerned to pay for the rectification of the fault, but was immediately reminded that there was no contractual relationship between them and thus (in the absence of negligence, which is always more difficult to prove than simple contractual liability) no liability arose.

Potential new owners thinking of entering into a contract for the purchase of a new boat through an agent may well consider entering into a collateral agreement with the builders.

This agreement would ensure that should the agent for any reason be unable or unwilling to perform his obligations under the express or implied terms of the main contract, then the builders will accept whatever liability would have attached to the agent. A simple exchange of letters between the purchaser and the builder to this effect will be sufficient to put the collateral agreement on a firm legal footing. A suitable draft letter for the builder to sign is given in Appendix 3.

Leasing schemes

Some builders provide a leasing facility for buyers which can have fiscal advantages. However the intending lessee should obtain an undertaking that the builder will in all respects regarding warranty claims treat the lessee as if he were the purchaser. Otherwise it may be possible for the builder to claim that it has no direct contract with the lessee, since it is the leasing company that is in fact the purchaser.

CONSTRUCTION OF A NEW YACHT TO ORDER

Throughout the previous chapters repeated reference has been made to the British Marine Federation standard form agreement for the construction of a new yacht. This contract, which was given the RYA seal of approval in 2000 is intended to be a fair compromise between the commercial needs of the builder and the aspirations of the purchaser.

Although many BMF members use this contract as a matter of course, a number of boatbuilders operate with their own less satisfactory standard form contract. Any individual considering having a new craft built to his order would be wise to insist on the BMF standard form being used, unless he is satisfied that the builder's own contract is no less favourable than that issued by the BMF.

The text of the agreement and accompanying notes are set out in Appendix 1 and 2; its conditions deal with the pitfalls that are most likely to occur.

Terms of payment

Although it is for the purchaser and builder to come to their own agreement on stage payments, it is worth bearing in mind that a normal pricing schedule would be a 5% or 10% first payment on the signing of the agreement, a 30% or 35% payment on completion of

the hull, a 40% payment on completion of interior joinery, installation of the engine or stepping of the mast, and the final 10% - 25% payment on completion of acceptance trials and signing of a satisfaction note by the purchaser. Different boats built of different materials will obviously merit consideration of different proportions of stage payments. The intention should be to allow the stage payments to reflect the actual value of the work and materials incorporated into the yacht at each stage.

An alternative approach on a large project would be to break the stage payments down according to the selling price less the builders profit to reflect the costs still payable to achieve completion at each stage.

In the case of a boatyard buying in a completed bare hull or a small boatyard undertaking a major project it may be that a higher first payment will be required to provide working capital for the purchase of materials and payment of the work force. There is an obvious risk attached to dealing with a yard on this basis and although some protection is given by clause 11 of the agreement, it would make sense to take out at least bankers' and accountants' references on a small builder before paying over a significant sum of money.

If the purchaser wishes the builder to guarantee the delivery date then damages for late delivery may be agreed (see page 7 above).

Buying for use on inland waters

Although there have been construction and equipment regulations in force on the River Thames since the mid-1920's regulations for privately-owned craft on waters controlled by British Waterways, and the Norfolk and Suffolk Broads Authority and other Environment Agency waters (the Medway and Anglian rivers) are a relatively new concept, and will need to be complied with if it is intended to base any boat on those waters.

The three navigation authorities, in co-operation with the British Marine Federation, have developed a training course and qualification scheme for inspectors. The intention being that a navigation licence or registration certificate will only be issued for craft that have a current certificate of compliance issued by an authorised inspector. The Boat Safety Scheme finally introduced in 1993 after lengthy consultation between the authorities is now compulsory on all British Waterways and Environment Agency waters.

Although the boatbuilder can be expected to know the exact terms of the standards, a prospective owner should also be aware of the requirements which are available on request from:

>British Waterways Board
>Willow Grange
>Church Road
>Watford WD1 3QA
>Tel: 01923 226422

>Environment Agency
>Recreation and Navigation
>Rio House
>Waterside Drive
>Aztec West
>Almondsbury
>Bristol BS12 4UD
>Tel: 01454 624376

Buying for commercial use

Reference has been made to regulations imposed by the Department for Transport (through the Maritime and Coastguard Agency) for commercially-used pleasure craft. Most of the Merchant Shipping legislation laying down rules for the design, construction and equipment of ships specifically exempts pleasure yachts or pleasure craft from compliance. However the Marques incident in 1985, in which a converted trading schooner capsized and sank with serious loss of life in a Tall Ships Race, led to the DfT amending the rules to exclude commercially used yachts from the exemption, and to require them to comply with a stringent Code of Practice. The regulations have been in force since 1994.

Yachts used bona fide for the private pleasure of the owner or his family or friends, or within a club syndicate, are exempt, provided that any contribution to costs is for running expenses only. Any charters, whether crewed or bare-boat, bring a yacht within the new regulations, (unless the charter is primarily for racing purposes), and indeed any other commercial purpose also necessitates compliance with the Code of Practice. The regulations have been in force since 1994

The regulations cover various areas of operation in five categories

ranging from less than 20 miles from a safe haven, to unrestricted service, and encompass all aspects of design and equipment, including stability requirements, weather-tightness, requirement for a diesel engine, detailed electrical arrangements, fire prevention requirements, and life-saving and safety equipment.

Many of these requirements are expensive to comply with, and undoubtedly go far beyond what has conventionally been considered adequate for cruising yachts in the past. Any prospective owner considering subsidising his costs by occasional chartering (let alone running the yacht on a full-time charter basis) should study the Code of Practice in detail with the builder, and draw up detailed costings of the additional construction and equipment requirements, before entering into a binding contract to buy the yacht.

Details of the Code of Practice for craft up to 24 metres can be obtained from:

> The Maritime and Coastguard Agency
> Spring Place
> 105 Commercial Road
> Southampton SO15 1EG
> Tel: 02380 329100

BUYING FOR OVERSEAS DELIVERY

Until the end of 1992 it was possible for a UK resident to purchase a yacht for immediate export overseas (the Mediterranean coasts of France, Spain and Italy being the most popular destinations), thereby avoiding any VAT payment. With the arrival of the single fiscal European Union area in January 1993, this means of tax avoidance is no longer available in any EU State.

For an EU resident wishing to base his yacht outside the EU area, it is still possible to avoid payment of VAT, provided that it is not intended to visit EU waters at any time. Thus Turkey, Morocco or even the Channel Islands remain popular as yacht tax havens, although a Jersey based yacht may be rather limited in its choice of non-EU cruising destinations.

For owners wishing to base their yachts in other EU States, VAT must now of course be paid. If it is intended to remove a new yacht to another EU State within two months of supply, VAT is not payable at the time of supply but will have to be paid in the EU country of destination at the rate applying to that country. VAT rates still vary considerably throughout the EU, with some Member States applying

very high luxury rates to larger boats. Buyers should check the current rates carefully before exporting a new boat - See Appendix 4.

The procedure for tax-free removal to another EU State involves the completion and signing of a declaration to certify that the yacht will be removed to another State. The seller will then send a copy of the declaration to HM Customs, who will inform the tax authorities in the destination country.

Buyers who prefer to pay VAT in the UK rather than the destination State, can do so buying in the ordinary way in the UK and then delaying export until the yacht no longer qualifies as new under EU tax rules. This involves keeping the yacht in service in the UK for more than three months and using it under its own power (or sail) for more than 100 hours.

These rules only apply to yachts over 7.5 metres in length. Smaller yachts must have the applicable VAT paid on them in the country of purchase even if it is intended to export immediately to another EU State.

As we have seen, VAT-free export to a non-EU State is still possible by virtue of the Sailaway Boat Scheme. This necessitates a prior arrangement with the builder and HM Customs, and requires the yacht to be removed from the UK within 2 months of the date of delivery. Once a VAT zero-rated yacht has been removed from the UK and it is intended to maintain its VAT-free status, it may not return to the UK or anywhere else within the EU while under ownership of an EU resident except by prior arrangement with the local customs authorities for the purpose of repair or refitting.

The fact that the yacht is being exported does not in any way affect the owner's rights under the Sale of Goods Act. Where a breakdown or component failure occurs, for which the builder is liable, the owner is entitled to have the repair carried out locally (having first discussed the problem with the builder and given him the opportunity of coming to remedy the fault himself) and to claim compensation for the costs of repair and any other associated losses.

The original VAT receipted invoice must be held safe along with all other title documentation to the yacht in order to facilitate its eventual onward sale.

RECREATIONAL CRAFT DIRECTIVE

Most people will be aware that importing a yacht from overseas will involve payment of VAT and Import Duties but many forget the requirement for the yacht to comply with the Recreational Craft Directive. Lack of awareness of this requirement can prove to be extremely costly.

The purpose behind the RCD is to allow a single European market in recreational craft to operate.

Since 16th June 1998 all recreational craft with a few exceptions, such as craft intended solely for racing, between 2.5 and 24 metres in length, sold or put into service in the European Economic Area (EEA) for the first time must comply with the essential safety requirements of the RCD and must be CE marked to certify compliance. This includes imported yachts either new or secondhand, and home built yachts if placed on the market within five years of completion, intended for sports and leisure purposes. The builder/his agent or the person importing the boat is responsible for compliance and marking.

The EEA includes all EU countries plus Iceland and Norway. A list of EEA countries can be obtained from the Technical Unit of the RYA.

A yacht that comes within the scope of the RCD must have accompanying documentation. These include a Technical File and an Owner's Manual which must include a written Declaration of Conformity. The yacht should also carry a CE compliance plaque in a prominent place.

The amending directive

The amending directive is intended to allow a single European Market in recreational craft to operate whilst maintaining a high level of environmental protection.

The amending Directive has been agreed (2004) and is set to apply to a wide variety of new recreational craft, including sail cruisers over a certain size, motor cruisers, motor boats and personal watercraft, whether powered by outboard, stern drive, or inboard engines. The changes will also apply to existing craft and their engines that undergo major modification and conversions.

It introduces a further set of essential safety requirements which include requirements as to emissions.

EU Member States must comply with most of its measures from 1st January 2005. However there is a further transitional period of 1st January 2007 in relation to compression, four-stroke ignition engines and two-stroke ignition engines.

Both Directives are enforced by Trading Standards Departments of Local Authorities. Breach of either of the Directives may result in a fine of up to a maximum of £5,000 and/or three months imprisonment. It is therefore imperative that the prospective buyer ascertain the yacht's RCD status prior to entering into a contract with the builder/agent.

For further detailed information on the RCD contact the RYA Technical Unit on 02380 604201

INSURANCE

Although yacht insurance in this country is not compulsory, there is so much scope for damage to the yacht, the crew, or other vessels in the ordinary course of navigation that it would be foolish not to have comprehensive insurance cover.

Unlike the simple form of contract used in household and motor car insurance, the standard yacht insurance policy is a complex document. It is difficult for the layman to understand the contract fully without access to the Marine Insurance Act 1906 and the body of marine insurance case law contained in the Lloyds law reports.

The yacht insurance market is highly competitive, divided between a number of Lloyds underwriters (who may be approached through an agency or via Lloyds brokers) and insurance companies (who may be approached either through Lloyd's or non Lloyd's brokers or direct). In the insurance market as anywhere else you get what you pay for,

and while it always pays to shop around you should not be tempted to go for the underwriter or company offering the lowest premium for that reason alone. Experience has shown that underwriters and companies away from the cheaper end of the market tend to be more flexible in interpreting the strict terms of the policy in the case of difficult claims, and speedier in settling the more straightforward claims.

With the wide variety of companies, brokers and underwriters competing in the market, and the great range of policies and policy wording being offered, it is sometimes difficult to make valid comparisons on a value-for-value basis.

When a broker is approached for a quotation, he will usually quote a figure between 0.5% and 1.5% of the declared value of the craft.

There is always room for negotiation over premium rates, as the nature of the risk varies according to a number of factors. Is the mooring secure against extremes of weather, is the area patrolled by police or harbour officials to discourage vandalism and theft? What is the intended cruising range? Does the owner have any significant qualifications? Has the craft been built to current BW or EA standards (and does the insurer regard that as relevant)? Is the owner prepared to carry a reasonable excess? (An agreement to pay the first £500 can make a big difference to the premium), or is he a member of a club that entitles him to a discount?

Most underwriters will be happy to insure a new yacht, or any yacht up to 10 years old, without a survey being required.

In all cases it is essential when completing the proposal form to put in the fullest and most accurate information and to answer all the questions literally. The proposal form constitutes the basis of a binding contract, and in the event of a claim being made, most underwriters will re-examine the proposal to ensure that the claim is valid within its terms of reference. The law recognises that insurance contracts are one-sided; the boat owner knows everything about himself, his boat and the nature of his proposed use of the boat. Since the insurer only knows what the owner chooses to tell him, he is protected by the principle of uberrima fides. Roughly translated this means that the insured must show the *utmost good faith* in providing information, failure to do so may entitle the insurer to avoid the contract even if a subsequent claim is irrelevant to the subject matter of the false statement.

So far as the average UK-based boat owner is concerned, there are three main cruising ranges available at standard prices which must be declared on a proposal form, these are:

(a) non-tidal waters within the UK;

(b) coastal cruising within an agreed range of the yacht's home port or permanent mooring;

(c) full coastal and sea-going cruising within the *home trade* limits, which cover all UK waters and continental coasts from Brest to Elbe, (some policies may include continental inland waters as far south as Paris, but an additional premium is usually payable).

Particularly in the case of fast motor boats (insurers normally attach special conditions to boats capable of 17 knots or more) security against theft, or against the weather while at a mooring or at anchor is a major concern to insurers. They will usually insist that if a trailed boat is not kept at home, it must be made secure in a locked compound, and if left afloat unattended, must at all times be on a secure and reasonably sheltered mooring.

Unlike motor insurance, there the value of a car in the event of a write-off is taken to be its current market value, marine insurance is usually based on the principle of agreed value. If a yacht is insured for, say, £10,000, and in the case of a total loss, the insurers are able to show that it would have fetched no more than £8,000 on the open market, they are still liable to pay the full figure. Provided the insured has not deliberately mis-stated the value, there should be no argument on the matter. This does not of course exempt him from accurately stating the price paid on the proposal form; this is not necessarily the same as the value of the yacht, although insurers may wish to know the reason for any difference in these figures.

Underwriters will of course need to be informed of any intention to use the yacht for charter, whether bareboat or skippered, or for any commercial purpose. While this is not a problem in itself, underwriters will normally lay down conditions about the qualifications and experience of prospective charterers.

Under the speedboat clauses in most policies, any use for racing or speed trials is specifically excluded, and special insurance should be taken out with the club organising any such event.

Difficulties can arise when an owner forgets to lay up (or re-launch) his yacht on the date stated on the proposal form.

Claims have been turned down on the grounds that the nature of risks while afloat are very different to those ashore. While most insurers are flexible about varying lay-up and re-launch dates, it is wise to inform them in advance of any proposed variation.

It is advisable to ensure that the policy includes cover for salvage claims.

So far as third party liability is concerned, with effect from May 2004, most standard policies provide the owner with indemnity up to £2m, or in some cases £3m. The RYA currently (2004) recommend third party liability cover at a bare minimum of £2m. It should be remembered that these high figures will rarely be approached, even in the case of a bad accident, as the Merchant Shipping Act Limitation of Liability provisions will normally apply. The effect of the limitation is to allow a yacht owner (or his insurers) to limit liability for third party property damage to about £360,000, and for death or personal injury to about £720,000. However, since limitation does not apply to guests or passengers injured aboard the insured's own craft, it is as well to carry adequate insurance against such misfortune.

An increasing number of harbour boards and navigation authorities are imposing third-party insurance requirements, and this trend is likely to continue over the next few years. In this context an important aspect of the cover provided is the cost of raising and removing the wreck of an insured boat in the event of it sinking in the fairway of a harbour or in the main channel of a navigable river or canal.

REGISTRATION

The 1956 Geneva Convention on the High Seas provides that ships take the nationality of their owners, while Articles 91 and 92 of the United Nations Convention on the Law of the Sea provides that States must issue documents evidencing the right of each ship to fly the flag of the owner's state while on the high seas or in foreign territorial waters.

Since a yacht (whether sail or power) falls within the definition of ship in the UK Merchant Shipping Acts, the provisions of the conventions and of UK Merchant Shipping legislation apply as much to yachts as to cargo ships or passenger liners.

Although it is not obligatory to register a yacht used only in UK waters, any yacht going overseas either permanently or for short cruises should be registered under one of the two registration schemes available to British owners.

The Small Ships Register first came into effect on 1st November 1983.

Now re-established under the Merchant Shipping Act 1995 as the Part III Register, it is intended to be an inexpensive and simple means of providing a documentary link between the owner and the yacht, the document being internationally accepted evidence of the nationality of the yacht.

The Part III registered yacht is as British as the Part 1 registered yacht and, by international convention, the Part III Certificate of Registry is as acceptable world-wide as the Part 1 Certificate of Registry.

What the Part III does not do however is:

(a) Provide documentary evidence of title or ownership of the yacht. (This could be a disadvantage when you come to sell the yacht, as a prospective purchaser could feel unsure about your unencumbered title).

(b) Offer the facility of registering a marine mortgage, which has the effect of protecting a lender's interest by impeding the transfer of title when the boat changes hands so long as the mortgage or charge remains uncleared. (A registered mortgage is often demanded by finance houses as a condition of lending money on the security of a yacht).

For all other purposes including:

(a) the shipping of bonded stores on yachts going beyond the Brest/Elbe limit;

(b) (for yachts over 7m in length) the wearing of privileged ensigns by Permit issued by an entitled yacht club

Part III provides an effective alternative to Part 1 registration.

Entry on the Part III Register also enables an owner to fulfil the registration condition for the grant of a permit to wear a privileged ensign (when the owner is a member of a privileged club) and also enables bonded duty-free stores to be shipped out of the country on voyages beyond the limits designated by HM Customs and Excise for this purpose.

For a yacht to be registered she must be less than 24 metres in length and owned by a person or persons (not a company) being ordinarily resident in the UK including:

(a) British citizens or nationals of an EU State who are established in the UK;

(b) British Nationals (Overseas);

(c) other Commonwealth Citizens.

The procedure for the Part III Registration requires a simple application to the Registrar General, on the appropriate form including:

(a) description of the vessel;

(b) overall length;

(c) name of the vessel;

(d) name and address of every owner;

(e) declaration that the owners are eligible to be owners of a British Ship, and that the ship is entitled to registration.

The application should be sent to the Registrar with the current fee (£12 for a 5-year certificate in 2004).

A registration certificate will normally be issued with no further formality required, and the owner must, within a month of registration, paint or fix on a visible external surface of the vessel the number of registration with the prefix SSR. This should be done in contrasting colour, in letters and numbers 30mm high and 25mm wide, typically above the rudder stock or the inside aft cockpit coaming in the case of a conventional sailing yacht, or on the wheelhouse door in the case of a conventional motor yacht. However, provided the marking can be readily seen, there is no specific rule as to its position.

As with Part I, the registration is for a 5-year period, and, if not renewed, the vessel will be removed from the Register after that time.

> Small Ships Register
> Registry of Shipping and Seamen
> PO Box 420
> Cardiff CF24 5XR
> Tel: 02920 448800

Part 1 registration

Part I Registration is the only option available if:

- the vessel is over 24 metres, or
- the vessel is company owned, or
- a person or company lending money on the security of the vessel requires a marine mortgage to be registered against it.

Entitlement to Part I Registration is limited to ships owned by one of the following:

(a) British citizens or persons who are nationals of an EU State who are established in the UK;

(b) Bodies corporate incorporated in any EU State;

(c) Bodies corporate incorporated in any relevant British Possession and having their principal place of business in the UK or in any such possessions;

(d) Citizens of British Dependent Territories, British Overseas Citizens and, British Nationals (Overseas).

In addition, an unqualified person may be one of the owners of a registered ship if a majority interest in the ship is owned by qualified persons. Where the owner or owners are not resident in the UK, the vessel may only be registered if a representative person, or company

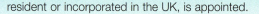

resident or incorporated in the UK, is appointed.

The procedure for Part I Registration requires an application to the Registrar General, in person or by post, accompanied by:

(a) a declaration of ownership and eligibility;

(b) evidence of title going back at least 5 years, including all relevant Bills of Sale and builder's certificate;

(c) the proposed name (which may not duplicate any name already on the Part I Register);

(d) the proposed Port of Choice selected from the list of 110 previous ports of registry (supplied with the application form);

(e) full details of the vessel and owner.

The application must also be accompanied by a measurement report, certifying the vessel's tonnage, general description, and specification.

For yachts under 24 metres a simplified form of measurement is permitted, which can be carried out by RYA appointed tonnage measurers.

For craft in excess of 24 metres a more complex measurement procedure is required which must be carried out by an authorised qualified surveyor.

Following receipt of all relevant documentation and the current fee (£130 for new registrations in 2004) the Registrar will issue a carving and marking note to the owner requiring (in the case of a private vessel under 24 metres) the newly issued Official Number and registered tonnage to be marked on the main beam or, if there is no main beam, on a readily accessible visible permanent part of the vessel either by cutting-in, centre punching, or raised lettering, or engraved on a metal, wood, or plastic plate permanently attached with lost head screws. The name and Port of Choice must be marked (either in black, white or yellow letters contrasting with the hull colour) conspicuously on the stern.

For craft under 24 metres, the owner must then certify that the vessel has been properly marked by returning the certified carving and marking note to the Registrar within 3 months. He will then be issued with a registration certificate. The Registrar will retain at his office copies of the builder's certificate (if any) and Bills of Sale, as well as the other documentation required for registration.

Prior to 1994, registration on the British Register was valid indefinitely, with the result that many thousands of ships of all sizes which had long ago ceased to exist, or been sold overseas, still remained on the Register. The regulations now provide for a 5-year registration term, for both new and existing registrations, and require that ships that are not re-registered at the appropriate time will be removed from the register. The Registrar issues a renewal reminder three months before expiry.

> Registry of Shipping and Seamen
> PO Box 420
> Cardiff CF24 5XR
> Tel: 02920 448800

OBTAINING A MOORING

Much has been written in recent times about the shortage of mooring space in this country. This has been brought about by an increase of between 3,000 - 4,000 yachts built and imported each year, restrictive planning policies by local authorities controlling the development of new marinas, and the need of new yacht owners to find a mooring near large centres of population.

In fact there is ample space in our creeks, estuaries, rivers and harbours to provide moorings for twice or three times the present numbers of small craft. The situation in certain defined areas is admittedly very tight; in the Solent area it is difficult to find a marina berth on a 12 month licence on the mainland, but for those prepared to look a little further afield, to Poole, the Isle of Wight, along the Sussex coast or further West there is much less pressure, with the further bonus of sailing in uncrowded waters.

Elsewhere around the coast many of the more popular small harbours have reached capacity, or unfairly restrict the grant of mooring licences to local residents. There will however always be space and normally at a much lower cost in the less accessible and less obvious areas and harbours. Unless you are intent on joining a keen racing fleet, or are very short of time to spend on travelling to your mooring, you should consider a mooring away from the most congested and expensive areas.

Looking further afield many boat owners have chosen marina berths on the Mediterranean coasts of France and Spain, and claim that in doing so they are saving money and have more time for sailing. With cheap flights available from airports throughout the UK to areas with marina berthing available at one third to one quarter of the fees charged in the UK this can make a lot of sense, even taking into account the fact that VAT-free export to another EU State ceased to apply after 31st December 1992.

Owners wishing to keep their new craft on a marina will find most of the options in the RYA *Marina Guide* published annually and accessible on the RYA Website.

APPENDIX 1
POINTS TO CHECK BEFORE SIGNING CONTRACT

1. How much can you afford to lose in case the builder/agent goes broke before the boat is delivered? Will he provide a bank guarantee?

2. How much is paid to builder/agent before buyer has title? Remember - in some contracts terms can work out at 100%. In the case of a yacht built to your personal order, do the proposed stage payments fairly reflect the costs of material and labour, and the profit element incurred by the builder at each stage in the construction? Is the builder prepared to allow a retention for some months to back up his guarantee as to defects that may arise after the acceptance trials?

3. In the case of a new build, is the builder using the standard form BMF contract (2000 edition) approved by the RYA. If not, then employ a lawyer or contact the RYA Legal Department to vet the contract the yard is offering.

4. Does the contract specify the boat and its equipment to your satisfaction eg:

    - is it to be the same as the demonstration model you have seen?

    - is the engine make and model to be the same?

    - are the make and description of sails to be the same?

    - are the deck fittings and other equipment to be the same?

5. Is the seller guaranteeing the specification of the hull (as to materials and construction details) and is there a guarantee against osmosis for a reasonable period?

6. Is the price fixed?

7. Do late additions to the extras list carry any penalty?

8. At what stage does the boat actually become yours? Remember that under some contracts you may have paid for 100% of the basic boat but, because extras are still being fitted the boat may still not be yours. Will the builder agree to mark all bought-in equipment and machinery with your name as soon as it is delivered to his yard?

9. If the worst comes to the worst and a liquidator is appointed, how will you identify your boat in the yard? Marking the hull with the name at an early stage is a useful safeguard.

10. Is the supplier prepared to guarantee a delivery date? Is he prepared to refund part of the purchase price on a pro-rata basis for late delivery?

11. Is there a cancellation clause? What does it say so far as the company is concerned and the customer is concerned?

12. If buying through an agent is a collateral agreement with the builder in place? (See Appendix 3).

13. Do you have a copy of plans, wiring and plumbing diagrams?

14. Examine yard history, try to find happy customers for references or ask the yard to put you in touch with previous buyers.

15. Consider paying a local experienced party or surveyor to keep an eye on yard works, otherwise be sure to visit regularly at intervals of less than 14 days in order to keep conditions of 1.2 on BMF standard form contact open to you.

16. Have you seen evidence of Builders' insurance?

17. Do you have an inventory of all equipment to be provided?

18. If you are buying a boat from stock, will the company provide evidence that any stocking finance or marine mortgage has been paid off?

APPENDIX 2
BMF/RYA BOAT BUILDING CONTRACT

Build Number/Hull Identification No./Boatmark No.

THIS AGREEMENT is made the   day of

BETWEEN

1. [   ] a limited company incorporated in England (Reg.no. No.)/Scotland (Reg.no. No.)/Northern Ireland (Reg.no. No.)/a sole trader/a partnership whose registered office/principal place of business is [   ] (the Builders)

AND

2. [   ] of [   ] The Purchaser

(jointly the Parties)

1 Agreement and specification of the boat

1.1   The Builders agree to construct and the Purchaser agrees to buy the boat described in the Specification as set out in Schedule 1, together with any drawings and plans, all of which shall be signed by the Parties, (*the Boat*) and in accordance with the terms of this Agreement.

1.2   Subject to any agreed amendments to the Specification, drawings and plans, the Purchaser shall have the right to reject any workmanship, materials and/or equipment which does not comply therewith. Such rejection shall be ineffective unless confirmed to the Builders by notice in writing within 14 days.

1.3   The Builders shall be under no contractual or other obligation to accept any order of the Purchaser until it has been confirmed and signed on behalf of the Builders by their authorised representative.

1.4 The Builders shall build the Boat in compliance with all applicable statutory requirements and regulations relating to the construction and sale of the Boat in the European Union or any other requirements or regulations which may be agreed in writing between the Parties.

2 Modifications and changes to the specification

2.1 No modifications or changes to the Specification, Delivery Date and/or price shall be binding on the Parties unless and until set out in writing and signed by both Parties.

2.2 The Builders shall have the right to refuse to agree to any modification or change to the Specification or Plans.

3 Contract price and payment

3.1 The price of the Boat is the amount set out in Schedule 2 together with the cost of any modifications or changes to the Specification agreed between the Parties under Clause 2.1 and any adjustments made under Clause 3.3 and, if applicable, VAT at the rate applicable from time to time (*together the Contract Price*). The Purchaser agrees to pay the Contract Price by installments as set out in Schedule 2 (*Stage Payments*) and as provided in this Clause.

3.2 The Builders shall give the Purchaser 14 days' notice of the anticipated date of completion of each stage of construction as provided in Schedule 2. On expiry of such notice the Purchaser shall certify that the stage has been satisfactorily completed (such certification not to be unreasonably withheld) whereupon the relevant Stage Payment will become immediately due and payable in full without discount, deduction or set off.

EITHER - Delete one of the alternatives to Clause 3.3 (see Notes for Guidance)

3.3 If during the period of this Agreement there is an increase in the Builders' net costs of constructing the Boat, whether in relation to materials or labour or which arises from any change in the applicable law or regulations, and provided always that the Builders have proceeded with reasonable despatch, the Parties agree that the Builders shall be entitled to increase the Contract Price proportionately to such increase in cost and the Purchaser undertakes and agrees to pay the Contract Price as so adjusted.

OR

3.3 Save as provided in Clauses 2.1 and 3.1 the Contract Price shall not be subject to any increase.

3.4 If the Contract Price is varied in accordance with Clauses 2.1 and/or 3.1 the Builders shall be entitled to require payment of any increase in the Contract Price by reason of any modification or change in full at the time of agreement thereto or, at their option, to receive such increase by way of additions to the Stage Payments.

3.5 If the Contract Price is varied in accordance with Clause 3.3 the amount of the increase shall be divided by the number of remaining Stage Payments and the amount so calculated shall be added to each remaining Stage Payment and Schedule 2 shall be amended accordingly.

3.6 If for any reason any tax, levy, charge or any other sum required to be paid by law shall be omitted from the amount of the Contract Price or shall be varied or introduced after the date of this Agreement and shall be required to be paid by the Purchaser the Purchaser shall pay such additional sum forthwith on demand.

4   Unpaid installments

4.1 If the Purchaser fails for any reason to pay the full amount of any Stage Payment or other sum due to the Builders on the due date the Builders shall be entitled to stop construction of the Boat until all outstanding payments have been paid in full, and the Delivery Date shall be extended by the period of such delay in payment.

4.2 If such failure to pay any sum due continues for 14 days the Builders shall thereafter be entitled to charge interest at 4% over Barclays Bank plc base rate, or the Builders' current commercial overdraft rate if higher, after as well as before judgement, calculated from the date upon which such payment became due and payable.

4.3 After a further period of 14 days' delay the Builders shall, without prejudice to any other rights, be entitled:

    4.3.1 to require payment from the Purchaser forthwith of the balance of the Contract Price then outstanding and to complete the construction of the Boat; or

    4.3.2 to terminate this Agreement and to sell the Boat pursuant to Clause 10.2.

4.4 The Purchaser shall in addition be liable for any loss or damage, special, direct, indirect and/or consequential losses incurred by the Builders as a result of the delay in the payment of the Stage Payments or any other sums due hereunder.

5 Acceptance trial and delivery

5.1 The Boat shall be completed and ready for delivery at the place and on the date stated in Schedule 3 or on such later date as may be determined in accordance with the terms of this Agreement (*the Delivery Date*).

5.2 Unless otherwise agreed between the Parties the Boat shall at the Builders' expense be taken on a trial trip (of not more than [ ] hours' duration) before delivery (*the Acceptance Trial*). The Builders shall give the Purchaser at least 14 days' written notice of the place and approximate duration of the Acceptance Trial, but if the date shall not be convenient to the Purchaser the Parties shall agree an alternative date not more than one month after the date proposed by the Builders.

5.3 If during the Acceptance Trial any defects in workmanship or materials or deviations from the Specification are found, the Builders shall forthwith rectify such defects or deviations and shall carry out a further Acceptance Trial in accordance with Clause 5.2.

5.4 If the Purchaser fails to attend a first Acceptance Trial, the Builders shall carry out a further Acceptance Trial pursuant to Clause 5.2, save that the cost thereof shall be for the account of the Purchaser.

5.5 If the Purchaser fails to attend such further Acceptance Trial, or if the Parties shall fail to agree an alternative date for a first or further Acceptance Trial, the Builders shall confirm in writing to the Purchaser that an Acceptance Trial has been deemed to have taken place and provided that the Builders shall certify that the Boat is constructed in accordance with the Specification and performs satisfactorily the Purchaser shall be deemed to have accepted it.

5.6 At the satisfactory conclusion of the Acceptance Trial the Purchaser shall sign the Certificate of Delivery and Acceptance in the form provided in Schedule 4. The final balance of the Contract Price shall become due and payable immediately upon signature of the Certificate of Delivery and Acceptance or upon provision by the Builders to the Purchaser of the Certificate referred to at Clause 5.5 or upon the Purchaser's wrongful failure or refusal to sign the Certificate of Delivery and Acceptance.

5.7 The Purchaser shall take delivery of the Boat immediately upon signature by the Purchaser of the Certificate of Delivery and Acceptance and payment of the final balance of the Contract Price and any other sums owing to the Builders by the Purchaser. If the Purchaser fails to take delivery of the Boat or fails to pay any outstanding sums due to the Builders then, in addition to any other rights which the Builders may have, the Builders shall be entitled to require the Purchaser to pay such reasonable berthing and/or storage charges as the Builders shall notify to the Purchaser together with any other expenses reasonably incurred by the Builders, including but not limited to insurance, maintenance and lifting of the Boat in or out of the water until actual delivery shall take place.

5.8 The Purchaser and the Builders expressly agree that the Builders shall not be responsible for investigating or otherwise ensuring that the Purchaser is competent and experienced in the proper control and/or navigation of the Boat. The Royal Yachting Association will if requested by the Purchaser provide a list of boat handling/training establishments.

6 Delays and extensions of time (force majeure)

6.1 If construction of the Boat is delayed directly or indirectly due to any cause beyond the Builders' reasonable control the Delivery Date shall be extended by the period of time during which such delaying event operates.

6.2 The Builders shall give the Purchaser written notice of any event in respect of which the Builders claim to be entitled to an extension of time:

    6.2.1 within 7 days of its commencement, stating the date on which the delay commenced, the cause of it and its estimated duration; and

    6.2.2 within 7 days of its end, stating the date on which it ended and the total period of the extension sought.

Any dispute arising between the Parties as to the operation of a delaying event shall be adjudicated in accordance with Clause 14.1.

6.3 If the Builders' premises, plant, machinery or equipment shall be so damaged by the operation of a delaying event for which the Builders are not responsible so as to make it impracticable for the Builders to complete the construction of the Boat, the Builders may, at their option (to be exercised within 21 days of the operation of the delaying event), cancel this Agreement by notice in writing to the Purchaser, whereupon the Purchaser shall be entitled by written election either:

    6.3.1 to take over and complete the Boat without further liability on the Builders whereupon the Purchaser shall pay to the Builders all sums then due, whether by way of Stage Payments or otherwise; or

    6.3.2 to require repayment of all installments paid by the Purchaser to the Builders and upon such repayment title in the Boat and all materials and equipment appropriated to the Boat shall revest in the Builders.

7   Access to boat and builders' premises

7.1 The Purchaser shall have the right to inspect the progress of construction of the Boat from time to time during the Builders' normal business hours with the prior written consent of the Builders, such consent not to be unreasonably withheld provided always that the Builders shall be entitled to appoint a representative to accompany the Purchaser or Purchaser's agent and that access shall extend only to those parts of the

Builders' premises necessary for the inspection of the Boat and/or the materials and equipment appropriated thereto.

7.2 The Purchaser shall observe all current rules and regulations applied by and to the Builders, and to their premises.

8 Warranties

In addition to the Purchaser's statutory rights the following warranties shall apply:

8.1 Subject to the conditions set out below and otherwise expressly set out herein the Builders warrant to the Purchaser that the Boat will be of satisfactory quality and reasonably fit for the purpose(s) made known to the Builders in writing prior to the date of this Agreement whether or not such purpose is one for which the Boat is commonly supplied and will correspond with the Specification and any variation, addition or modification thereto. The Builders further warrant that the Boat will be free from defects in materials and workmanship for a period of 12 months from the time of delivery.

8.2 The Builders warrant to the Purchaser that on delivery the Boat will comply with:

8.2.1 all legislative requirements and regulations relating to the sale of the Boat in the European Union for any purpose(s) made known under 8.1 above; or

8.2.2 any other requirements or regulations which may be agreed in writing between the Parties.

8.3 The Purchaser's statutory rights and the warranties set out in Clauses 8.1 and 8.2 shall be subject to the following conditions:

8.3.1 The Builders shall have no liability for any defect in the Boat arising from the Specification supplied, provided or varied by the Purchaser;

8.3.2 The Builders shall repair or replace any defect in the workmanship, materials or equipment or their failure to correspond with the Specification. Such repair or replacement shall be carried out by the Builders at their premises or, where that is not convenient to the

Parties, the Builders shall pay the reasonable cost of having the work carried out elsewhere;

8.3.3 The Builders shall only be liable for any defects or failures which were not apparent on reasonable inspection during the Acceptance Trial or within a reasonable time thereafter;

8.3.4 The Purchaser shall notify the Builders in writing immediately on discovery of any alleged defect and the Builders or their agent shall have the right to inspect the Boat including the right to carry out sea trials to enable the Builders or their agent to examine or assess the extent of the alleged defect. The expense of any such trials shall be borne by the Builders if the defect is shown to be one of workmanship or materials.

9 Insurance

9.1 The Builders shall insure the Boat (together with all equipment and materials installed or intended for it and within the Builders' premises) in the joint names of the Builders and the Purchaser from the date of this Agreement until the date of delivery.

9.2 Such insurance shall be effected with a reputable insurer for a sum equal to the replacement cost of the completed Boat (to a maximum of 125% of the Contract Price) and shall include the cost of any additions or variations to the Specification which have been agreed between the Parties.

9.3 Such insurance shall be on terms no less favourable than the Institute Clauses for Builders' Risks applicable from time to time. Documentary evidence of such insurance, its terms and conditions and proof of payment of the premium shall be provided to the Purchaser on request.

9.4 In the event that the Boat, equipment or materials sustain damage at any time before delivery any monies received in respect of the insurance shall be receivable by the Builders and shall be applied by them in making good such damage in a reasonable and workmanlike manner and the Delivery Date shall be extended by such period as shall be reasonably necessary to effect the necessary repairs. The Purchaser shall not be entitled to reject the Boat, equipment or materials on account of such damage or repairs or to make any claim in respect of any resultant depreciation save that where the Boat is declared an actual or constructive total loss the Purchaser shall have the option, to be exercised within 28 days of the loss, of cancelling this Agreement in which event the insurance money to the value of Stage Payments already paid shall be paid direct to the Purchaser by the insurers and the Purchaser will abandon all rights under the said insurance to the Builders. This Agreement will thereupon be determined in all respects as if it had been duly completed and the Purchaser shall have no further right to claim against the Builders.

9.5 If the Builders fail to provide satisfactory evidence of insurance in accordance with the provisions of this Clause, the Purchaser shall be entitled to insure on comparable terms and to deduct the amount of the premium actually paid from the Contract Price.

10 Termination

10.1 The Builders shall be entitled to terminate this Agreement by written notice without prejudice to any other rights or remedies available if:

10.1.1 the Purchaser becomes insolvent; or

10.1.2 the Purchaser has failed without good reason to make one or more Stage Payments or any other payment within 28 days of such payment being due and payable and has not referred the underlying reason for such delay to dispute resolution under the provisions of Clause 14.

10.2 If the Builders exercise their right to terminate this Agreement under Clause 10.1 they shall be entitled to sell the Boat, the materials and the equipment and/or any other property of the Purchaser in the possession of the Builders for the purpose of the construction of the Boat. The Builders shall give the Purchaser 28 days' written notice of their intention to sell the Boat and/or other property and such notice shall give details of the reasons for the sale including details of any sums due and payable to the Builders together with details of the proposed method of sale. Following the sale of the Boat and/or other property the Builders shall repay to the Purchaser the balance of the proceeds of sale after deduction of all sums owing to the Builders and all reasonable legal or other expenses including, but not limited to, the costs of sale and maintenance and storage charges incurred by the Builders.

10.3 In addition to any other rights set out herein the provisions of the Torts (Interference with Goods) Act 1977 (the Act) shall apply in relation to uncollected boats and/or other property and for the purposes of the Act it is hereby expressly agreed that the Builders' obligations to the Purchaser as custodians of the Boat and/or other property terminate upon the expiry or lawful termination of this Agreement and pursuant to the Act the Builders have a right of sale exercisable in certain circumstances as set out in the Act.

10.4 For the purposes of Clauses 10.2 and 10.3 only the Purchaser hereby irrevocably appoints the Builders as the agent of the Purchaser for the sale of the Boat and/or other property. The Purchaser shall co-operate with the Builders insofar as may be necessary to effect a sale of the Boat including signing or confirming any authority or instructions.

11 Ownership of the boat

11.1 The Boat and/or all materials and equipment purchased or appropriated from time to time by the Builders specifically for its construction (whether in their premises, upon the water or elsewhere) shall become the property of the Purchaser upon the payment of the first Stage Payment or, if later, upon the date of the said purchase or appropriation. The Builders shall, however, have a lien on the Boat and any materials or equipment purchased for or appropriated to the construction for recovery of all sums due (whether invoiced or not) under the terms of this Agreement or any variation or modification hereof. Any materials or equipment rejected by the Purchaser shall forthwith revest in the Builders.

11.2 The Builders shall, insofar as it is reasonably practicable to do so, mark all individual items of equipment and materials which are purchased for or appropriated to the construction of the Boat.

11.3 The Purchaser shall not without the prior written consent of the Builder which consent shall not be unreasonably withheld sell, assign, pledge or otherwise put a charge on the Boat by way of security for any indebtedness prior to delivery except for the sole purpose of obtaining a loan to finance the construction of the Boat. If the Purchaser charges the Boat in breach of the terms of this Clause, the balance of the Contract Price shall forthwith become due and payable without prejudice to any other rights or remedies of the Builders. The Purchaser shall not have the right to assign or transfer this Agreement or any of his rights and obligations hereunder without the prior written consent of the Builders.

11.4 If the Purchaser is in breach of any of the terms of this Agreement after the property in the Boat and/or materials and equipment has passed to him and the Builders wish to exercise their rights to sell the Boat and/or materials and equipment as set out herein then the property in the Boat and/or materials shall revert from the Purchaser to the Builders following 28 days' notice by the Builders of their intention to exercise such rights.

11.5 Notwithstanding the provisions of this Clause risk in the Boat shall remain with the Builders until the actual delivery of the Boat to the Purchaser.

12 Copyright

Any copyright or similar protection in manuals, drawings, plans, specifications, including the Specification prepared by the Builders or their employees or agents, shall remain the property of the Builders.

13 Notices

Any notice required to be given hereunder shall be in writing and either (i) given by hand with proof of delivery or electronic transmission confirmed forthwith by first class pre-paid post, or (ii) sent by first class pre-paid post to the other party at the address set out in this Agreement or such other address in the UK as may have been notified by the other party.

14 Dispute resolution - law and jurisdiction

14.1 If during the construction of the Boat any dispute arises either as to an adjustment of the Contract Price pursuant to Clause 3.3 or as to when a Stage Payment is due and payable or as to the operation or duration of a delaying event or whether for the purposes of the policy of insurance the Boat has suffered substantial damage, then, and without prejudice to the Parties' rights to litigate such dispute, it may be referred to a single surveyor who shall be independent of the Builders and the Purchaser and whose identity and terms of reference shall be agreed by the Parties or, in default of agreement, by the President for the time being of the Yacht Designers and Surveyors Association. The surveyor so appointed shall act as an expert and not as an arbitrator and his written decision shall be final and binding upon the Parties and his fees and expenses shall be borne equally by the Parties.

14.2 This Agreement shall be construed in accordance with English law or where the Builders have their principal place of business in Scotland in accordance with Scottish law and the High Court of England or Scotland (as the case may be) shall have exclusive jurisdiction in respect of any dispute or other matter arising hereunder.

15 Interpretation

15.1 The construction of this Agreement is not to be affected by any headings.

15.2 References in this Agreement to the Parties shall include their respective successors and permitted assigns save where such succession or assignment is expressly prohibited by the terms of this Agreement.

15.3 This Agreement forms the entire agreement between the Parties and unless specifically agreed in writing by the Builders no warranty, condition, description or representation is given or to be implied by anything said or written in the negotiations between the Parties or their representatives prior to this Agreement.

15.4 If the Builders are a member of a group of companies the Builders may perform any of its obligations or exercise any of its rights hereunder by itself or through any member of its group provided that any act or omission of any such other member shall be deemed to be the act or omission of the Builders.

15.5 In this Agreement words importing the masculine gender also include the neuter and feminine gender and words importing the singular include also the plural.

15.6 Reference to any legislative provision includes a reference to that provision as amended extended or re-enacted and any replacement thereof (either before or after the date of this Agreement).

15.7 If any term or provision in this Agreement shall be held to be void in whole or in part under any enactment or rule of law such term or provision or part shall to that extent be deemed not to form part of this Agreement but the validity and enforceability of the remainder of this Agreement shall not be affected.

16 Variations and additions

This Agreement is subject to the variations and additions set out below or identified below and attached to this Agreement and initialled and dated by both Parties.

Signed for and on behalf of the Builders

In the presence of:

Full name of witness

Address

Occupation

Signature

Signed for and on behalf of the Purchasers

In the presence of:

Full name of witness

Address

Occupation

Signature

N.B. (1 Witness in England, 2 in Scotland)

Schedule 1 - Specification

The Specification for the Boat is as set out below or as identified below and attached to this Agreement and signed by the Parties.

Schedule 2 - Stage payments

Contract Price

The Boat £

Plus VAT (if applicable) £

Price inclusive of VAT £

The Contract Price shall be payable by Stage Payments as set out below

1) Upon signing of this Agreement £

2) Upon the hull being available at the Builders' premises fully moulded, planked, plated or formed and confirmed in writing to the Purchaser by the Builders £

3) Upon substantial completion of the fitting of the interior joinery work or installation of the engine or stepping of the mast whichever is the earlier £

4) Upon completion of the Acceptance Trial and the signing of the Satisfaction Notice by the Purchaser or upon deemed acceptance and completion of the Builders' Certification as provided in Clauses 5.5 and 5.6 £

Schedule 3 - Delivery

Delivery Date
Place of Delivery

Schedule 4 - Certificate of delivery and acceptance

Place of Acceptance Trial
Date of Acceptance Trial
Persons present at Acceptance Trial

I the undersigned hereby certify that the construction of the Boat and the Acceptance Trial have been completed to my reasonable satisfaction.

Subject to the terms of the Agreement dated [   ] this Certificate of Delivery and Acceptance will not affect my statutory rights should the Boat or its equipment subsequently prove to be defective.

Signed by [   ], the Purchaser

Dated

Notes

These are explanatory notes only and, although very important, do not form part of the agreement itself.

1. This form is published by the British Marine Federation (BMF) and approved by the Royal Yachting Association (RYA).

2. It is a simple form of agreement designed for the leisure marine market and cannot be expected to cater for every unforeseen circumstance arising between the parties. It is considered be the RYA and the BMF to strike a fair balance between the interests of purchaser and the builders. Certain aspects of this agreement can be used for transactions between commercial parties.

3. It should be completed in duplicate, taking care to insert the appropriate details on pages 1 and 2. Any specification, drawing or additional clause which cannot be accommodated on the agreement should be firmly attached to the agreement and signed by both parties. Additional clauses inserted on page 8 should be initialled by both parties.

4. Both parties should sign (in the presence of a witness in Scotland).

5. The Certificate of Delivery and Acceptance must be signed by the purchaser or his agent on delivery and acceptance of the completed craft.

6. The box at the top of page 1 is for the builders' use. It is recommended that the identification number should be marked on all materials and equipment intended for incorporation in the craft.

7. If it is of great importance to the purchaser that the craft should be delivered by the date specified on schedule 3, then this section should be completed.

8. (a) Clause 3.3 to 3.6 is a price variation clause which allows the builders to adjust the price to reflect inflation occurring between the dates of the agreement and the final installment falling due. The clause should be deleted where the parties agree on a fixed-price contract, (usually where the period between signing and final payment is likely to be short).

   (b) Builders are reminded that the clause does not permit a price increase to reflect inflation occurring between original quotation and signature of the agreement. For this reason builders should express their quotation as valid for a limited period and, if necessary, should revise them where the agreement is signed after that period.

   (c) The clause allows builders to increase the price so as to reflect all increases in the Retail Prices Index occurring after the date of the agreement. If they intend to rely on the clause, builders should base the price on current costs without the addition of any inflation factor.

9. If the purchaser leaves or arranges for others to leave any item on the builders' premises or on the craft, he should insure the item himself unless the builders expressly agree in writing to do so. Builders should in any event carry adequate insurance cover against claims arising from their negligence which result in damage to any property on their premises.

10. Statutory Rights - Nothing in this agreement shall affect the consumer's statutory rights, which rights include conformity with any description or sample, satisfactory quality and fitness for any stated purpose.

11. Additional copies of this agreement may be obtained from

   British Marine Federation
   Marine House
   Thorpe Lea Road
   Egham
   Surrey TW20 8BF
   Tel: 01784 473377

   or

   Royal Yachting Association
   RYA House
   Ensign Way
   Hamble
   Southampton
   Hampshire SO31 4YA
   Tel: 02380 604100

APPENDIX 3

Draft letter of indemnity from builder on agency purchase.

Dear Mr Buyer

YOUR PURCHASE OF A THUMPER 28' FROM A.N. AGENT LTD. (The Agent)

In consideration of your agreeing to purchase a Thumper 28' from the agent, and in the event of the agent being unable to perform his obligations under the express or implied terms of the agreement, Thumper Yachts Ltd hereby undertakes to accept whatever legal liabilities would have attached to the agent under that agreement.

Thumper Yachts Ltd

APPENDIX 4

2004 European Community VAT rates

AUSTRIA	VAT at 20%
BELGIUM	VAT 21% on new or imported boats. First Registration tax of 25M ECU payable on new boats above 7.5m. Registration tax of 2500 ECU decreasing by 10% per annum payable on resale.
CYPRUS	VAT at 15%
CZECH REPUBLIC	VAT at 22%
DENMARK	VAT payable on full value of boat when dealer is involved in transaction in force. VAT rate 25%. Light and navaid tax based on 1% of insurance value in force.
ESTONIA	VAT at 18%
FINLAND	VAT at 22%.
FRANCE	VAT at 19.6%. Tax on all users of inland waterways under consideration. Annual user tax based on engine power greater than 5hp and hull size (greater than 3GRT) in force.
GERMANY	Tax on dealer's margin in force. VAT on new boats 16% in force.
GREECE	VAT at 18%
HUNGARY	VAT at 25%
IRELAND	VAT at 21%.
ITALY	VAT at 20%
LATVIA	VAT at 18%
LITHUANIA	VAT at 18%
LUXENBOURG	VAT at 15%
MALTA	VAT at 18%

NETHERLANDS	VAT at 19%
POLAND	VAT at 22%.
PORTUGAL	VAT at 19% for all types of boats. Annual tax depending on length and engine power.
SLOVAKIA	VAT at 19%
SLOVENIA	VAT at 20%
SPAIN	VAT at 16% on all boats plus a 13% registration tax on boats over 7.5m. This is compulsory for Spanish nationals and to all others who wish to register their boat in Spain.
SWEDEN	VAT at 25%
UK	VAT at 17.5%

Promoting and Protecting Boating

The RYA is the national organisation which represents the interests of everyone who goes boating for pleasure.

The greater the membership, the louder our voice when it comes to protecting members' interests.

Apply for membership today, and support the RYA, to help the RYA support you.

Benefits of Membership

- Access to expert advice on all aspects of boating from legal wrangles to training matters
- Special members' discounts on a range of products and services including boat insurance, books, videos and class certificates
- Free issue of certificates of competence, increasingly asked for by everyone from overseas governments to holiday companies, insurance underwriters to boat hirers

- Access to the wide range of RYA publications, including the quarterly magazine
- Third Party insurance for windsurfing members
- Free Internet access with RYA-Online
- Special discounts on AA membership
- Regular offers in RYA Magazine
- ...and much more

Join now - membership form opposite

Join online at www.rya.org.uk

Visit our website for information, advice, members' services and web shop.

① Important To help us comply with Data Protection legislation, please tick *either* Box A or Box B (you must tick Box A to ensure you receive the full benefits of RYA membership). The RYA will not pass your data to third parties.

☐ A. I wish to join the RYA and receive future information on member services, benefits (as listed in RYA Magazine and website) and offers.
☐ B. I wish to join the RYA but do not wish to receive future information on member services, benefits (as listed in RYA Magazine and website) and offers.

When completed, please send this form to: RYA, RYA House, Ensign Way, Hamble, Southampton, SO31 4YA

**② **

Title Forename Surname Date of Birth   Male Female

1. ☐☐ ☐☐☐☐☐☐☐☐☐☐☐☐ ☐☐☐☐☐☐☐☐☐☐☐☐☐☐☐ DD/MM/YY ☐ ☐
2. ☐☐ ☐☐☐☐☐☐☐☐☐☐☐☐ ☐☐☐☐☐☐☐☐☐☐☐☐☐☐☐ DD/MM/YY ☐ ☐
3. ☐☐ ☐☐☐☐☐☐☐☐☐☐☐☐ ☐☐☐☐☐☐☐☐☐☐☐☐☐☐☐ DD/MM/YY ☐ ☐
4. ☐☐ ☐☐☐☐☐☐☐☐☐☐☐☐ ☐☐☐☐☐☐☐☐☐☐☐☐☐☐☐ DD/MM/YY ☐ ☐

Address

Town County Post Code

Evening Telephone Daytime Telephone

email Signature: _____ Date: _____

③ Type of membership required: *(Tick Box)*

☐ **Personal** *Current full annual rate £33 or £30 by Direct Debit*
☐ **Under 21** *Current full annual rate £11 (no reduction for Direct Debit)*
☐ **Family*** *Current full annual rate £50 or £47 by Direct Debit*

* *Family Membership: 2 adults plus any under 21s all living at the same address*

Please see Direct Debit form overleaf

④ Please tick ONE box to show your main boating interest.

☐ Yacht Racing ☐ Yacht Cruising
☐ Dinghy Racing ☐ Dinghy Cruising
☐ Personal Watercraft ☐ Inland Waterways
☐ Powerboat Racing ☐ Windsurfing
☐ Motor Boating ☐ Sportsboats and RIBs

Instructions to your Bank or Building Society to pay by Direct Debit

Please complete this form and return it to:
Royal Yachting Association, RYA House, Ensign Way, Hamble, Southampton, Hampshire SO31 4YA

Originators Identification Number

| 9 | 5 | 5 | 2 | 1 | 3 |

5. RYA Membership Number (For office use only)

To The Manager: Bank/Building Society

Address:

Post Code:

2. Name(s) of account holder(s)

3. Branch Sort Code

4. Bank or Building Society account number

6. Instruction to pay your Bank or Building Society
Please pay Royal Yachting Association Direct Debits from the account detailed in this instruction subject to the safeguards assured by The Direct Debit Guarantee.
I understand that this instruction may remain with the Royal Yachting Association and, if so, details will be passed electronically to my Bank/Building Society.

Signature(s)

Date

Banks and Building Societies may not accept Direct Debit instructions for some types of account

Cash, Cheque, Postal Order enclosed £
Made payable to the Royal Yachting Association

077 | **Office use only:** Membership Number Allocated

Office use / Centre Stamp